T0329374

THE INFLUENCE OF SEA POWER
ON THE HISTORY OF THE
BRITISH PEOPLE

The Lees Knowles Lectures on Military History for 1947

THE INFLUENCE OF SEA POWER
ON THE HISTORY OF THE
BRITISH PEOPLE

BY

ADMIRAL SIR W. M. JAMES, G.C.B.

CAMBRIDGE
AT THE UNIVERSITY PRESS
1948

CAMBRIDGE
UNIVERSITY PRESS

University Printing House, Cambridge CB2 8BS, United Kingdom

Published in the United States of America by Cambridge University Press, New York

Cambridge University Press is part of the University of Cambridge.

It furthers the University's mission by disseminating knowledge in the pursuit of education, learning and research at the highest international levels of excellence.

www.cambridge.org
Information on this title: www.cambridge.org/9781107645554

First published 1948
First paperback edition 2014

A catalogue record for this publication is available from the British Library

ISBN 978-1-107-64555-4 Paperback

CONTENTS

PREFACE

In the sailing era we could not wage war unless we won and held the command of the sea-lines of communication for the safe passage of troopships to disputed areas; to-day we cannot survive for more than a few weeks, let alone wage war, if that command is wrested from us and our flow of seaborne imports of food and raw materials ceases. The destructive power of war weapons and the speed of advance into battle have been continually increasing since the beginning of the century, but the merchant ship, on which our existence depends, still circumnavigates the world at a relatively slow speed.

From Tudor times the protection of the merchant ship, outward bound with troops or homeward bound with cargoes, has been the responsibility of the Royal Navy, but this responsibility was shared with the Royal Air Force in the last war. We cannot foretell what weapons will attack our trade routes in the next war and therefore what weapons we will require to defend them. If, however, we are to survive a future war, our weapons for commanding the sea routes must be capable of warding off all forms of attack, whether by surface vessel, submarine, mine, aeroplane or 'push-button' weapons. We must, as in the past, be able to exercise sea power.

The main theme of these lectures is that throughout history four elements have conferred the power to control the sea routes—merchant ships, bases, weapons and skilled men to wield those weapons—and that we have emerged victorious from ten major maritime wars because our enemies have lacked one of these elements. It is in the fourth element—leadership and fighting qualities—that we have on most occasions shown considerable superiority, and it was for this reason that I chose 'Nelson' as the subject of one lecture. For though he far outshone his contemporaries and predecessors they, too, were men of high moral courage, skilled strategists and tacticians, and could draw loyal and devoted service from their officers and men. Great fleets manœuvring in battle to the orders of one man, who can lose a war by one mistake, will probably never be seen again, but we will have need of men of the same character and personality as the Admirals of the great sail and steam fleets whatever weapons emerge from the scientific laboratories.

W. M. J.

April 1948

CHAPTER I

SEA POWER

In past years the purpose and value of lectures on the history and art of war have been unquestioned.

Knowledge of their rich war history and the achievements of their forebears on the battlefield has fortified the British people in times of adversity, and has often inspired men and women to acts of superb heroism. Until recently, the method of conducting war had been systematically developed to accord with the development of war weapons. The principles remained unchanged, and therefore the study of the methods employed in earlier wars was profitable and indeed essential, if on the outbreak of war our forces were to be deployed to the best advantage, and if the battle tactics employed by the force-commanders on land, sea and in the air were to be not just the fruit of sudden inspiration, but of knowledge of the tactics employed by the great commanders in the past.

But with the explosion of the first atom bomb over Hiroshima we seem to have come to the end of a chapter in the history of war. It is not the value of a general knowledge of our past history which is put in doubt. But of what value to-day is a detailed study of past wars, of what use a knowledge of the strategy and tactics employed for weapons of such comparatively insignificant striking power as armies, fleets and air forces, when the issue will be decided by the discharge of a few atom bombs?

To-day the value of lectures on war depends on the answer to that question. Obviously a study of past methods is of no practical value if, following a period of strained relations, those living far from our principal cities are awakened one morning by distant rumbling, and hear later in the day that London, Liverpool, Newcastle and Cardiff have been laid in ruins. But to say this is to assume that with the appearance of the atom bomb a chapter in the history of war weapons came to an end, and that for the first time in history the brain that conceived a new weapon could not conceive a counter-weapon.

In effect the history of weapon and counter-weapon began when a very ingenious prehistoric man stretched a skin on a forked branch to ward off the blows of his enemy. And in modern times the battle between shell and armour has been waged for over a hundred years; for periods the armour-makers produced armour which broke up shells on impact, and these periods have always been followed by periods when the shell has dominated. The advent of a new weapon has usually led to the belief that all other weapons are obsolete or obsolescent, but that belief has been short-lived. Once the enthusiasts have overcome the opposition of the scoffers and the wilfully blind, a new weapon has been rapidly developed and has acquired a dominating position, only to be overtaken in its turn by counter-weapons, and forced back into its proper place in the armoury.

In recent times the torpedo-boat, the submarine, the aeroplane and the tank have all been acclaimed as dominant weapons, against which older weapons were powerless. Yet each in turn has eventually been fitted into its proper place in the weapon-mosaic. No weapon has so far been forced out of the mosaic by a new weapon. The infantry soldier in Burma was sometimes fighting with the same weapons, and using the same tactics, as his predecessor of a thousand years ago.

There is, therefore, no proof that the brains which invented these new and terrible weapons are for the first time incapable of inventing a means of exploding them before they arrive at their objective. Let us remember that the fast-moving aeroplane was almost invulnerable to the anti-aircraft gun, but to-day the scientists are very nearly in sight of a projectile which will chase the plane, and when this is achieved the once dominant bombing plane will occupy a smaller portion of the mosaic. But if the belief that the atom bomb is the first completely dominant weapon is to prove ill-founded, then here is another reason for not abandoning the study of past wars.

Until the happy day when the peace of the world will be assured by a United Nations Organization, and until the existing weapons of war—armies, fleets, air forces—disappear, we of all nations cannot afford to scrap existing weapons, or be ignorant of how to use them if we are attacked. Our life-lines are the ocean trade-routes. If no ships arrive at our discharging ports for three weeks we cannot continue to live, let alone wage war. We are the most vulnerable country in the world. If, therefore, a nation bent on our destruction deploys existing weapons—ships, planes—on our trade-routes, and if we have no means of driving off those ships and planes, then we will be on our knees asking for terms three weeks after the declaration of war. A few warships disposed off the St Lawrence, the Plate, and at some focal points on the main sea-routes could arrest all our shipping. Why blacken and destroy your enemy's country when abject surrender can be extracted without firing a shot? There is here an unanswerable argument for maintaining defence forces composed of weapons which seem to be out-dated by the atom bomb, and concurrently an un-answerable argument that there is still value in studying the methods of conducting past wars.

We have always been an unwarlike nation of warriors. We have always hated war and resented its wastefulness in life and wealth. To drag money from Elizabeth to pay for the fleet was like getting blood from a stone. And if for Pitt's name you substitute that of Neville Chamberlain in the pages of Arthur Bryant's *Years of Endurance* de-scribing the political manœuvres prior to the outbreak of the French Revolutionary War, you can fancy you are reading about the months before the outbreak of the Second World War.

We have only once been fully prepared for war—for the First World War—and that was because every man, woman and child in this country could understand our danger when the Germans announced their intention of building a fleet to challenge our maritime supremacy.

We have usually begun a war ill-equipped and only able to deploy forces in strength much inferior to our enemy; but we have usually emerged victorious because our officers and men have been imbued with the warrior spirit, have endured what Kipling aptly called 'the sodden years of heaped up weariness' with greater fortitude than the enemy and never lost their battle efficiency, and because leaders of vision, skilled strategists and tacticians have never failed to appear sooner or later. It is because we have always been an unwarlike nation that we do not think or talk about war until war is upon us—and thereby we have often courted disaster.

During the First World War Lord Esher wrote:

Why do we worry about history? Julian Corbett writes one of the best books in our language upon political and military strategy. All sorts of lessons, some of inestimable value, may be gleaned from it. No one, except perhaps Winston, who matters just now has ever read it. Obviously history is written for schoolmasters and armchair strategists. Statesmen and warriors pick their way in the dark.

It is noteworthy that the most brilliant and important strategic decision of the Second World War—the decision to accept great risks to build up a strong defence in Egypt—is ascribed to Mr Churchill and to his lifelong study of war. In contrast, this is what Lloyd George wrote:

After the Battle of Jutland Admiral Jellicoe came to the conclusion it was not safe for his imposing Armada of enormous Dreadnoughts to undertake prolonged operations to the South of the Dogger Bank, as the risk of mines and submarines was too formidable. They were not to enter the North Sea unless they were forced to do so by direct challenge from the German High Sea Fleet. Meanwhile the Flagship must be interned in safe creeks, and the flag had to be carried on small craft, the nimbler destroyers and the weather-beaten trawlers. Here is the 'Nelson Touch' up-to-date. There was an atmosphere of crouching nervousness.

No one who had made a rudimentary study of past maritime wars could have written that. There was no 'crouching nervousness'. Jellicoe was acting exactly as Nelson would have acted. The 'Nelson Touch' does not connote foolish haphazard operations with no object. Nelson would never have attempted a close blockade if his enemy could use some weapon which would steadily reduce the strength of a blockading fleet. Like Jellicoe he, too, would have relied on a distant blockade, the only disadvantage being less certainty of knowing when the enemy sailed.

We should never forget that if pressure on the Admiralty to reduce the strength of the Grand Fleet, in order to free potential for other services, had succeeded, we might have lost the war. A defeat of our main fleet would have been followed by the collapse of the whole system of seaborne trade defence. But it is not only statesmen and leaders who can profit from some knowledge of past wars and the influence of sea power on our history; our people would not have been so vulnerable to propaganda if they had had even an elementary knowledge. An example is the campaign between the two World Wars to convince the people that the aeroplane had rendered obsolete all other weapons; if the Cabinet Committee set up to examine the claims had not kept their heads and recommended a continuance of shipbuilding we would have been able to hold out only about as long as Poland did. Other Powers were astonished at the success of this campaign; their response was to speed up their shipbuilding. Another example was the claim that all that was necessary to win the war was to bomb Germany: millions were convinced that the Army would never have to land on the Continent. We ran dangerously close to *losing* the war because priority was not given to the defence of the trade-routes. How foolish we would have looked if our planes had all been grounded for want of petrol which failed to arrive because there were insufficient planes to counter the activities of the submarines. It seems strange now that anyone should have thought that the mere lengthening of the reach and raising of the destructive power of weapons had altered the whole process of making war. It should surely have been obvious that the last stage would necessarily be the landing of an army which would eventually occupy and police Germany, and that that army would have to land under the cover of bombardment. The bombardment of back areas had been immensely stepped up by air-bombing, but the principles had not altered.

To sum up this preamble. The time has not yet come either when war is unthinkable or when victory will go to the nation that is first off the mark with atom bombs. A study of past wars is not a sterile occupation, and a people who have even a rudimentary knowledge of war are less vulnerable to propaganda about armaments. They are better able to appreciate the necessity for devoting some of the nation's income to defence, they understand the reasons for the allocation to various defence services, and above all they are aware that our sea-lines of communication are our life-lines: sever them, and we are sunk.

Sea power can be very simply defined. It is the power that enables its possessor to send his troops and trade across the water which lies between nations and the objects of their desires, and to prevent his opponent from doing so.

More simply still—control of the sea. Four elements confer this power—fighting instruments, bases, merchant shipping, competent seamen. These were the elements 2500 years ago. Whenever one of these elements has been lacking, attempts to exercise sea power have failed. Failure to recognize that inexorable fact has on more than one occasion jeopardized our prospects of gaining the victory, and has frequently brought defeat to our enemies even when in one element—in fighting instruments—they have been far stronger.

In olden times the Athenians were well aware of the importance of sea power. The Athenian army was not as strong as some of the neighbouring armies; but embarked in ships and striking where and when it chose it was a powerful instrument of war. And Athens, thanks to her command of the sea, was able to draw from overseas—iron, hemp, wax, copper, flax and timber—and to prevent her enemies from obtaining these essential commodities. Athens exercised sea power because she had good fighting ships propelled by oars, a large number of merchant ships, good bases and seamen. This was, of course, not organized war at sea, which is of comparatively modern origin. The method of conducting sea war in ancient days has been aptly described as 'cross-ravaging'. It was centuries later, when the sailing ship replaced the oared galley, that the increase in radius of action extended the influence of sea power—and sea power became of interest to our Lancastrian kings.

They had few opportunities of exercising sea power, and a Navy List of 1417 gives the British fleet as three great ships—*Jesu, Trinity Royal, Holigost,* six carracks—*Peter, Paul, Andrew,* etc., and six smaller ships. Judging from pictures they must have been very unhandy and difficult to manœuvre. They mounted only small guns, but were probably as efficient as contemporary warships built in Europe.

Even in those early days the habit of forgetting the importance of sea power to an island state as soon as danger passed (that habit which has so often nearly caused our elimination as a great Power) had become a settled one, and by 1452 the only ships in the Royal Navy were the *Trinity* and *Holigost,* both rotting and useless. But in the next century the spirit of adventure which stirred the English people under the Tudor kings brought with it an awakening to the importance of sea power. Merchant adventurers were seeking fresh markets in Russia, Persia, the west coast of Africa and the West

Indies. At the same time Spain was acquiring a monopoly in the West Indies, and the Portuguese and Dutch were concentrating their energies on the East Indies and South America.

It was Henry VIII, in a preamble to the many Acts of navigation which were passed at that period to foster the building of ships, who said that an island environed by the sea 'could conduct its trade by no other road but the sea and that ships and seamen were a great defence and surety of the Realm in time of war'.

On 13 June 1514, the sum of 6s. 8d. was paid for the hallowing of a ship launched at Erith. She was called *Henry Grace à Dieu*. She was far more powerful than any other ship in existence, being between 1000 and 1500 tons and mounting twenty-one guns—cannon, demi-cannon, culverins, sakers and falcons.

One of the best-known drawings is, I believe, here at Cambridge in the Pepysian collection. Though previous to this launch small navies had been built and then allowed to fade away, the launching of that ship heralded a new era. The Tudors understood sea power. To-day it seems just common sense that Drake should be sent to attack the shipping in Spanish ports which it was known was being prepared for the invasion of England, but at that date such a lengthening of the striking power of the Navy was a new departure. Then again the operations of Hawkins and Frobisher on the Spanish sea-lines of communication to the Indies was also a new use for the fleet; we see in it the seeds of blockade, with ships remaining at sea and cruising in strategic positions. Command of the sea-lines had become a definite object. Yet when the Armada was defeated Spain was not beaten, because one of the elements was lacking. England had fighting ships, merchant ships and seamen, but no bases from which to keep up pressure on Spanish trade. On the other hand the element lacking in the Armada was seamen. It was lack of bases that severely limited the power of the large navy commissioned by the Commonwealth. Indeed, Cromwell sent off an admiral to search the Mediterranean area for suitable harbours. But it was not until Charles II received Tangier as a portion of his Portuguese bride's dowry that a base was made available in those waters.

The great maritime wars with the Dutch, however, the inevitable result of two enterprising maritime nations competing for the carrying trade, were all fought out in the narrow seas. Both nations had built immense fleets, and in several of the battles each side assembled nearly one hundred ships. Great seamen were afloat—Tromp, de Ruyter, Blake, Monk. The battles—Dungeness, Kentish Knock, Portland, Lowestoft, Four Days' Battle —are not easy to follow, but it is evident in the first Dutch war that the protection of commerce deflected both belligerents from what should have been their chief purpose—the defeat of the enemy's main fleet.

In the second Dutch war—the last purely maritime war—the mistake was rectified, and something new in naval strategy emerged.

It was realized that the issue ultimately depended on the big fleets. Attack on commerce and blockade might force a decisive battle, but there would be no victory until the enemy's main fleet was defeated; trade losses would continue to even out until that battle was fought. The principles were thus slowly evolved from experience. It was the War of the Spanish Succession, whose maritime operations seem so colourless beside the masterpieces of Marlborough, that taught us much about trade protection—convoying trade through dangerous areas and maintaining squadrons at focal points—and, more important still, the immense power of the amphibious operation of landing an army on the enemy's coast at a selected time and place. The army under Peterborough, conveyed by the fleet under Shovell to Barcelona and Toulon, showed the immense possibilities of an amphibious operation—an operation possible only for the belligerent who holds full command of the sea.

At the opening of the eighteenth century Britain acquired the element that had so far been lacking—bases overseas. After the acquisition of Gibraltar in 1704 and Minorca in 1708 Britain's sea power could be exercised in all European seas. In the Seven Years War which opened in 1756 all the experience of earlier wars was reflected in the strategical handling of the British fleets. During those earlier wars there was some by-play in the distant oceans; there were raids and counter-raids, and invasions on a small scale. But now there were infinitely greater prizes, countries scattered over the world whose riches lay open to the maritime Powers. Who was to be master of the Indian Ocean, and control the destinies of India? Who of America?

The first shot at sea was fired by Captain Richard Howe, off Newfoundland; the first shot on land by a Colonial Major, George Washington, at Fort Duquesne, afterwards Fort Pitt and now Pittsburg. The stakes were great and the issue depended on the control of the sea-lines of communication. Recognizing that all forces engaged in protecting trade and conveying armies over-seas were operating under the protection of the main fleets, and that defeat of the main fleet would be followed by collapse of all effort involving ships, a powerful fleet under Hawke watched the main fleet based on Brest, whilst another fleet under Boscawen watched the Toulon fleet. That was the main commitment, and it was because the French fleets were thus contained that our troops and all they required in stores and reinforcements were able to make the Atlantic passage in security. It was this movement which culminated in Wolfe's famous opera-tion at Quebec, in the acquisition of Canada, and the capture of Havana and several West Indian islands.

It was also possible to send and nourish a fleet in the Indian Ocean, and it was the outcome of three stiff battles between Pocock and D'Aché which ended French pretensions to India. One of the outstanding features of this war was Pitt's exploitation of the amphibious opera-tion. Julian Corbett wrote: 'For Pitt, Army and Navy were the blade and hilt of one weapon, and from the moment the weapon was in his grip he began to demon-strate the force and reach of his method.' To the belli-gerent who held command of the sea an army embarked in ships which could be landed at any chosen place and time and re-embarked if and when desired proved an immensely powerful weapon, whose influence was out of all proportion to the actual number of ships and men employed. The earliest attempts were unsuccessful, because the generals and admirals were at loggerheads. But Wolfe, who was quartermaster-general at one of these failures, wrote a famous memorandum afterwards; and later in Canada, in co-operation with Admiral Saunders, he conducted the perfect operation.

This Seven Years War thus established certain strategical principles which have never since changed, although the weapons have so completely changed. In this war victory rested with the British forces because France lacked the fourth of the elements—seamen. There was little to choose between the belligerents in the other elements—number of warships, shipping, bases. Hawke's remarkable victory in Quiberon Bay in a storm could only have been achieved by a fleet manned by prime seamen.

After this most successful war the country rested on its oars and, despite the efforts of Hawke and Saunders, the legacy was dissipated. The fleet was allowed to rot away, and it was in no condition to meet the next call on it. This came when it was evident that the European maritime Powers would take advantage of the situation produced by the revolt of the American Colonists.

The British government made a fatal mistake at the outset in sending to America weak forces which were ignored—a mistake repeated in the Second World War when two capital ships were sent to the Far East to face the third strongest navy in the world. Once the Colonists were armed and steeled (by Washington) to fight and suffer hardships, only very powerful forces could have restored the situation. Pitt said truly: 'You may ravage; you cannot conquer; it is impossible. You cannot conquer the Americans. I might as well talk of driving them before me with a crutch.' But very soon this commitment in America became of little importance in face of the commitment for our all-too-small fleet that arose when France, Spain and Holland marshalled their powerful fleets to drive us off the ocean, and later to carry the war into these Islands.

The stage was once more the five oceans. On paper we should have been overwhelmed by weight of numbers, but once again the enemy lacked the fourth element— seamen. With the exception of Suffren, the French and Spanish admirals never showed any desire to force a decisive battle. They were content with half-begotten battles, and were deflected from what should have been their main object to some subsidiary object, such as the capture of an island. We were fortunate in our commanders, Howe, Rodney and Hood, though the irascible Rodney lost many opportunities because he was hated by his captains and would never take them into his confidence. 'My eye on my captains frightened them more than the enemy', wrote that disagreeable man. On the other hand we kept in command of the Home fleet old and incompetent admirals, and it was only because the French and Spanish admirals were older and more incompetent that the country was saved from invasion.

When in 1778 a great Franco-Spanish fleet of over seventy ships appeared in the Channel there was a British fleet of only thirty ships to bar its advance. But D'Orvilliers, who had written: 'I will run like an old man who is afraid of the cold and is unable to undertake a hard day's work', and Cordova, the Spaniard, who was seventy-five, and who was reported to have several defects inseparable from old age, were not the men for the occasion. That great fleet did nothing; jealousies, sickness, lack of purpose, continual councils of war robbed it of all its strength. How fortunate for us! Kempenfelt, the chief of the staff in the Channel fleet, wrote of the British commander-in-chief, Hardy:

The confused conduct here is such that I tremble for the event. A man who never thinks beforehand and is therefore under the confusion of a surprise when anything happens, always in such a hurry when he takes in hand to do anything that he never does it; puzzling himself and all about in little detailed minutiæ whilst essentials are never thought of. It is with the greatest difficulty I can ever prevail upon him to manœuvre the fleet; he is always so impatient and in such a hurry to get to the Westward, to the Northward or to the Southward that he won't lose time to form a line.

It is of interest that Hardy was given the appointment because his political views were agreeable to the government of the day. Howe and several other competent admirals were not employed because they were politically opposed to the government. 'Where is Lord Howe at this alarming period', wrote Kempenfelt. In parliament 'Give us Black Dick' was shouted—but the ministers were obdurate. We can be thankful that our effort in more recent times has not been weakened from that cause, but it is a warning of what may happen if British ministers put party before State.

At a later stage Russia, Sweden and Denmark commissioned their fleets and threatened to come against us if we exercised our full belligerent rights. We were quite alone. Our forces were very small compared with the forces ranged against us. Yet we survived, though we lost the American Colonies. It is an extraordinary story. The ineptitude of the French and Spanish admirals has been mentioned, but there were other causes of failure. The three main enemy forces, the Franco-Spanish European fleet, the Franco-Spanish fleet in the West Indies and the American army never worked in co-operation. If, from the outset, the European fleet had used its great strength to prevent the sailing of British squadrons, while at the same time the West Indies fleet had co-operated closely with Washington's army, British ministers would have been hard put to it to adopt any profitable countermeasures. Only once was close co-operation attempted, when de Grasse entered the Chesapeke, and then British dominion over the American Colonies came to an end.

From time to time the big Franco-Spanish concentrations in European waters had complete mastery if they chose to act, but the costly efforts ended in useless parades. The Spanish fleet was great in numbers and guns, but of little consequence. Major operations were frequently abandoned on account of heavy sick lists; the Spanish fleet suffered far more from the ravages of disease than from British guns. Our enemies had in rich measure all the elements except one: they lacked competent seamen. Their admirals had not taken to heart the strategical lessons of earlier wars, they had no tactical imagination, and were poor hands at keeping their ships seaworthy and battleworthy.

Though it was the days of the press-gang the smaller British fleets were manned by fine determined personnel, and commanded by fine seamen. We were even able to maintain a fleet under Hughes in the East Indies of sufficient strength to fight Suffren's fleet. Five fierce battles were fought, and the casualties in one battle were greater than those at Trafalgar. This campaign depended entirely on bases, and whoever occupied Trincomalee had a great advantage. We also sent an expedition to capture the Cape, in order to have a base *en route* to the Indian Ocean.

We had had a narrow escape, but once again we apparently believed, in the words of the Treaty, that peace would be universal and perpetual: and as a result interest in the sea forces waned. We were true to form, an unwarlike nation of warriors. So the fleet was at a low ebb in the early days of the French Revolution, and Pitt was determined to go to any lengths to avoid war. But, thanks to a breathing space whilst the issue of peace and war was in the balance, we had a strong fleet, on a war-footing, by the time the French government declared war. Once again we enjoyed the services of some splendid leaders—Howe, Jervis, Keith, Cornwallis, Bridport and later Nelson. Once again we stood alone with the forces of France and Spain actively ranged against us, and the fleets of Russia, Sweden and Denmark commissioned and holding a threat over our heads. On the other hand, the Revolution had wrecked the efficiency of the French fleet. Admirals and captains had disappeared in the holocaust. The ships were commanded by lieutenants and pilots hastily promoted. Our fleets keeping watch on the enemies' great fleets were nearly always inferior in numbers. Jervis with fifteen ships was at one time faced with thirty-eight. Keith with fifteen was operating against forty-eight. But leadership and strategical knowledge were lacking in these great enemy fleets and, more important, Bonaparte, perhaps the greatest master of land warfare, never understood maritime warfare. The issue in that long war was decided by British sea power and the maritime strategy was admirable throughout. When the British government learnt of great activity at Toulon, St Vincent—his title had been won by a heavy defeat of the main Spanish fleet, mainly due to a remarkable tactical move by Captain Nelson—was told to make this concentration his main objective. He sent a large part of his fleet under Nelson, then a rear-admiral, to watch Toulon. Bonaparte was extraordinarily successful in disguising the purpose of this concentration, and it was generally believed that Ireland was the objective. But it was an Eastern Empire that occupied his dreams, and the conquest of Egypt was his objective. It remained a dream, because after a long search Nelson sighted the French fleet in Aboukir Bay, and put into execution a brilliant tactical plan which all his officers understood.

Accepting the immense navigational hazard—he had only a rough pencil sketch of the shoals—he destroyed all except two ships. Thereafter the French army in Egypt was virtually marooned.

During the long search Nelson was at one moment within a few miles of the vast unwieldy French army on its way to Egypt. The weather was misty; Nelson had no frigates; and he never saw them. That was one of the decisive moments in history. If Nelson's compact and highly efficient fleet had attacked that ship-borne army there could have been only one end; Bonaparte, and a galaxy of generals who later became famous, might have been taken prisoners.

Bonaparte's skilful diplomatic moves to range the powerful Russian, Swedish and Danish fleets on his side were also brought to nought by Nelson. Hyde Parker was too old and staid for the Baltic campaign, but fortunately Nelson was his second-in-command. The destruction of the Danish fleet at Copenhagen put a stop once and for all to the warlike plans of the Northern Powers. But we were once again all alone. As the war progressed the French navy steadily increased, thanks to Bonaparte's driving power. But he could not make admirals, and it was his admirals who would not sail when he ordered them, nor fight as he wished them to. He conceived a grandiose strategical plan for the destruction of Great Britain. The Toulon fleet, the Brest fleet and the Roche-fort fleet were to evade the British watching fleets, and sail to the West Indies. After capturing the islands they were to concentrate and appear in overpowering force in the Channel, while the army of invasion crossed the narrow strip of water: 'Let us be masters of the Straits for six hours, and we shall be mistress of the world.'

But his plan went awry. It was strategically unsound; for he should have ordered his fleets to give battle to the British fleets, not try and evade them. He had some little difficulty in forcing Villeneuve to leave Toulon. When he did he slipped past Nelson's watching fleet; the long blockade became the long chase across the Atlantic, but the Brest fleet failed to evade. When Nelson arrived in the West Indies he was greatly inferior to Villeneuve, but the French admiral had no intention of fighting. As soon as he heard that the British fleet had been sighted he started off for Europe, with Nelson in chase. Nelson was too far behind to catch up. When he arrived at Gibraltar he had not been out of the *Victory* for nearly two years.

Once again the French were in a most favourable position, with big fleets at Brest, Rochefort and on the Spanish coast. But once again they fiddled; they did not achieve any big concentration that would have been a serious threat to British watching fleets, and Villeneuve took his fleet to Cadiz and incurred the wrath of his master. Nelson, having handed over his ship to the admirals on blockade, returned to England. But he was soon afloat again when Blackwood brought the news that the Franco-Spanish fleet was in Cadiz. Nelson took over from Collingwood the command of the fleet watching Cadiz, and at once explained to his captains the new battle tactics which he hoped would enable him to destroy the enemy's centre and rear whilst their van was unable to come to their aid. He had grave doubts if Villeneuve, despite his superiority in numbers, would give battle. He knew that Collingwood had prevented any merchant ships arriving, and that Cadiz could not for long feed the enormous number of mouths, but he feared Villeneuve would sail his ships by squadrons and evade. He did not know that Villeneuve, aware that an order from Napoleon to haul his flag down was on its way and that disgrace, if not worse, awaited him, had decided to attempt to restore his fortunes by a victory. So the two fleets met off Trafalgar. The new tactics were entirely successful, the combined fleet was shattered. Napoleon abandoned his invasion plans and ordered the armies on the Channel coast to strike camp and march eastwards.

It was not the end of the maritime war, but there was no more fighting on the grand scale. Britain held the command of the seas for the next ten years and so could pass an army oversea to the Peninsula and later across the Channel to Waterloo. It was British sea power that caused the downfall of Napoleon.

In this, the last of the wars of the sailing era, the belligerents were fairly evenly matched in two elements —shipping and bases. In fighting ships the British fleet was often in very inferior strength. It was in the fourth element, seamen, that the British enjoyed such immense superiority. Napoleon's strategical plans were unsound; he did not know how to wield sea power. Nevertheless, if his admirals had displayed even moderate ability as strategists and tacticians, and if the crews of the French ships had been only moderately good seamen, the British commanders would often have been hard put to it to maintain their stations and keep control of the situation.

There is something very pathetic in the Spanish admiral's description of his crews at St Vincent, and in Villeneuve's letter to Napoleon when a storm drove his ships back into Toulon.

The sailing era was thus the golden age of British naval supremacy, though that supremacy was not due to superior strength in ships afloat. It was this which enabled our forebears to spread British influence over the world. We have seen that the strategic principles of sea war were gradually evolved from experience, and that by the time the Seven Years War broke out it was clear that the issue depended on the main fleets.

Trade protection and trade attack, amphibious operations and nourishing armies overseas were only possible if the main fleet contained or defeated the enemy's main fleet. As already noted, the method of conducting the Seven Years War was the method of conducting both World Wars in our own century. We have seen too that sea power could only stretch its arms as far as the endurance of the ships would carry them. It was the acquisition of bases, first in the Mediterranean then in America and the West Indies, then the Cape and then in the East Indies, which enabled British sea power to be extended to all quarters of the globe.

In the Dutch wars and the Seven Years War the British fleet and the enemies' fleets were fairly evenly matched. In the War of American Independence and in the French Revolutionary War Britain stood alone against all the maritime Powers. It was that fourth element—seamen—which enabled her to avoid destruction, and instead emerge with credit.

Lastly, we have seen that we were never ready for war. Queen Elizabeth's hatred of spending money on armed forces was shared by all her successors. Being an unwarlike nation of warriors, we strove against being involved in war. But when war could not be avoided, seamen, superior to those of any other nation, appeared almost miraculously from seaports, villages and farms; and there were always men to take command of them who were richly endowed with all the gifts essential for the successful conduct of war at sea.

CHAPTER II

NELSON

In April 1941 German bombers wrecked Admiralty House, Portsmouth, and those other houses in the Royal Dockyard that were never suitable as substitutes. The *Victory* was lying in the old Tudor dock, miraculously untouched so far from bombing, an emblem of victory. No home in England could be more stately; no rooms so suitable for transacting the business of command as the spacious cabins under the poop. So for eighteen months I spent my days in the cabin that was once Hardy's and entertained my guests in Nelson's day- and dining-cabins. It was a romantic setting. It required little imagination to conjure up a picture of the ship in her full dress under all plain sails and studding sails. As a midshipman I had served as officer of the watch in a barque-rigged corvette in the South Seas and the singing of blocks and tautening ropes as the ship rose and fell in the long Pacific swell was still music in my ears. In the quiet of the evening, when the confused noise of hammers and pneumatic riveters, the shouting of men berthing ships, and the rattle of wheels on the cobbled roadways had died down, and only the strident screams of gulls quarrelling over a titbit of jetsam broke the silence, I often thought of her last voyage and could picture with some exactness the sailors eagerly racing one another up the ratlines to crowd on more sail, knowing that Nelson, their Nelson, was urgent to join the fleet off Cadiz. I could picture, too, the excitement when the look-out in the fore cross-trees reported that sails were in sight, and that moment when the yards were swung and every stitch of canvas spread for the approach to her last battle. Sometimes, but with less exactness, I made pictures for myself of those momentous hours between the time she took her place at the head of the weather line of battle and the time she lay shell-torn and with all her sails in ribbons surrounded by French ships which had hauled down their colours. All along the lovely sweep of deck were the very guns that had held off the concentrated attack of seven great French and Spanish ships, and then double-shotted had turned into dust and splinters the stern of Villeneuve's flagship.

Living in such surroundings, conjuring up so frequently its dramatic scenes, privileged to project myself into the past and spend brief, dreamlike periods with the goodly company who hauled the ropes, set the sails, and manned the guns through the long blockade, the long chase, and the last battle, I was inevitably seized with the desire to know more and more about the central figure of the drama. And so, walking that deck which he walked for two years without setting foot on shore, I went in search of Nelson. I re-read books about him and re-read his letters, and I knew that much of what I read was apocryphal. I felt certain that he would never have evoked that wonderful response to his leadership, that whole-hearted loyalty and affection, if he had been histrionic. The sailor of those days was no different from the sailor of to-day, he has never trusted or felt warm regard for officers who do not behave naturally. And I found I was right. There were two Nelsons: there was the Nelson who when in thrall to Emma Hamilton and being paraded around European Courts incurred strong criticism and some contempt for his behaviour; but whenever he was alone with other men, and free from the influence of Emma, he was always the same simple, rather boyish, fellow.

Walking that deck I could not believe the widely accepted view that he was a frail man always battling against illness; and again I found I was right. First-hand accounts of him during the Baltic campaign and the long blockade depict a man of remarkable vigour. Up at five every morning completing the business of the fleet and a heavy correspondence before noon: then lunch, a gay affair, with never less than eight or nine guests: followed by six or seven hours' walking exercise, whatever the weather, and early to bed. I found many instances of his extraordinary fortitude and physical endurance. After his arm was shattered at Teneriffe he insisted in helping men out of the water with his good arm and he was writing with his left hand the day after the amputation. He was up all night before Copenhagen drafting orders for every ship, yet he showed no signs of fatigue next day, one of the most strenuous and anxious of his life. He frequently spent days and nights on end in open boats in all weathers. The post-mortem report revealed that at forty-seven he was an exceptionally well-preserved man.

The belief that he was a frail man has arisen from his

habit of writing in exaggerated language about his health whenever he was depressed and there was no prospect of active work. His was the not uncommon case of the man whose mind and health invariably sympathize. The recipients of his gloomy forebodings, knowing his temperament, were sometimes worried about him but never alarmed.

I had a fair knowledge of his campaigns and battles when he was a flag officer but I had not before delved deeply into his earlier life. I had not realized what an extraordinary story, what a revelation of character, was to be found in those years of preparation for the responsibilities of high command.

There is value for all of us in a study of his life because he did not take the easy road, he did not obtain rapid promotion as a young man for war service or through influence; he owed his promotions to his qualities as a seaman and leader of men, and he suffered much disappointment and frustration before he set foot on the ladder of fame.

Therefore, I will try in a brief review of his career to throw into relief those incidents in his life which illustrate the moral strength that won for him the command of the principal fleet when his country was in peril.

The most powerful influence in his life was his strict religious belief. His faith, which never wavered from the time he sat at his father's feet in the Norfolk rectory, sustained him through all trials and tribulations. His abiding trust in his Maker is conspicuous in many of his letters, and we know from his chaplain that he never rose in the morning or went to bed at night without saying his prayers. The daughter of the vicar of Merton wrote: 'His residence at Merton was a continued course of charity and goodness, setting such an example of propriety and regularity that there are few who would not be benefited by following it.' This was a far greater and more powerful influence than the influence of Emma, about which so much has been written in recent years. Emma did not enter his life until after he had won the Battle of the Nile. Emma or no Emma he would have been appointed second-in-command to St Vincent after his return from the Mediterranean, and been detached for service in the Baltic and given command of the inshore squadrons at Copenhagen. His liaison with Emma only made it more difficult for the First Lord and St Vincent to make the appointment. Emma or no Emma he would have been chosen for the command of the fleet watching Cadiz. With the Nile and Copenhagen to his credit there was no other competitor.

Nelson was one of a large family and his father, a country vicar, was no doubt delighted when his brother-in-law Captain Suckling said he would take one of the boys to sea. That was in those days the method of entering midshipmen. Suckling was a very wise man, and sent his young nephew to a merchant ship for a year to learn the rudiments of seamanship. When he returned Suckling kept him employed in boats to learn the navigation of the Narrows. Many years later when, after Copenhagen, Nelson was in command of the anti-invasion forces, he expressed his gratitude for this training in the Narrows.

Then one day Nelson heard that an expedition was going to the Arctic. He immediately applied, but was told no boys were being appointed. He would not take no for an answer, but worried his uncle to such an extent that he gave in and Nelson was appointed to one of the ships. This is the first, and a very striking, example of the strength of his character. How few boys would have refused to take no? He returned a robust, active boy and went to the East Indies for two years. There, as has happened to so many, he was struck down by fever, but the voyage home restored his health and he was appointed midshipman to a battleship on convoy work in the Atlantic.

His captain, struck by his ability to command and his efficiency, made him one of the officers of the watch. Remember he was only a boy, and officer of the watch in a square-rigged ship was a very responsible position. He passed his examinations for lieutenant, and was appointed to a frigate in the West Indies. Here again his captain was so struck by his ability that he brought him to the notice of the commander-in-chief, Peter Parker, and he became third lieutenant in the flagship. Vacancies due to illness and war often occurred in those days, and in a short time Nelson became first lieutenant and executive officer of the flagship. This was a most responsible position; he had to keep the ship seaworthy, and to order the work of the ship's company. He did his work so well that Peter Parker seized the first opportunity of a vacancy to appoint him commander of a small ship. And in that ship again he did so well that after a few months he was promoted to captain, in command of the frigate *Hinchinbroke*. He was not yet twenty-one.

It is a most remarkable story. The War of American Independence had broken out, many of Nelson's contemporaries had been engaged in battle and in minor operations, but he had so far seen no active service. Yet by his outstanding qualities as a seaman and leader of men he was a captain before he was twenty-one.

Now came his first experience of active service. We know that the publicity attached to a war operation depends on what other operations are being conducted at the same time. Zeebrugge in the First World War attracted enormous publicity because nothing else was happening at the same time. The comparable operation against St Nazaire in the Second World War—an operation which achieved its object, whereas Zeebrugge achieved nothing—received little publicity because it was overshadowed by operations on the grand scale in other areas. So the Nicaraguan expedition, which was jointly commanded by Nelson and a soldier, was probably never heard of in London or even in the main fleets. The object was the destruction of the Spanish settlements; but in that fever-ridden country the expedition soon found that the principal enemy was disease and fever. There came a time when Nelson and a young officer were themselves loading and firing the field gun.

Nelson would probably never have returned from that expedition if Peter Parker had not seized another opportunity of advancing him. He was relieved by Collingwood, who incidentally had relieved him in his first command and who became his greatest friend—'Coll' as he always called him—but he was too ill to take up his new command and returned to England. When fit again for service he was appointed to another frigate on the North American station. One day Hood arrived at New York from the West Indies. The fighting had died down in North America but might flare up at any moment in the West Indies. Nelson, an unknown young captain, went on board Hood's flagship and asked him to take him back to the West Indies. That required great moral courage.

One of the officers of the flagship was Prince William, the future King William IV, and he wrote a most interesting account of the young captain who suddenly appeared on board. He describes his quaint appearance due to the cut of his coat and his hair, and then how the moment he began to speak he and Hood realized this was no ordinary young man; he was so eager, so knowledgeable about affairs.

Hood took him to the West Indies but the expected fighting did not occur and Nelson returned to England still with no war service.

Then he was appointed to another frigate and after some months of service in convoy work in the North Sea again sailed for the West Indies. There on the Leeward Island station he was soon involved in a difficult situation. He and Collingwood on their first cruise discovered there was a widespread 'black market' to which governors, commanders and their own commander-in-chief turned a blind eye. The British government, wishing to foster trade between Great Britain and Canada and the Indies, had issued definite instructions that there was to be no trade with America. Nelson found American ships in every port. He determined to stop the traffic. He was soon the most unpopular man in the Indies, and ostracized wherever he went. He was a gay and sunny natured young man, he was extremely popular wherever he went and much in request at parties, and now he had to endure long months of ostracism during which he seldom set foot on shore. When he found that he could not win his battle single-handed he took the remarkable course of writing direct to the First Lord of the Admiralty and the King. I think this is the most striking incident in his life. This young unknown captain wrote direct to the King; and the letter was effective.

It was whilst under this cloud of enmity from the British residents in the Indies that he met and fell in love with Fanny Nesbit. It is obvious from the letters that it was not a passionate attachment, but they were in love with one another, a love that endured until after the Battle of the Nile. When he was badly wounded at the Nile and thought he was dying, he exclaimed "I am killed, remember me to my wife."

He returned to England, and for the next six years lived the life of a country gentleman in Norfolk.

He soon knew that he was in disfavour at the Admiralty, that many influential people whom he had antagonized by putting down the 'black market' had not forgiven him, and to his dismay his requests to be appointed to a ship on the two occasions when the fleet was mobilized were refused. He thought that his naval career was ended.

Then to his joy the postman brought the letter he had so long awaited. The French Revolutionary War had broken out and he was appointed to a battleship. He had always found the ships he was appointed to were the finest ships in the service and their ships' companies the finest ships' companies: and now when he joined the *Agamemnon* again he was delighted with his ship and his ship's company.

He joined Hood in the Mediterranean. Hood had not forgotten him, and on every opportunity gave him independent command. He was the senior naval officer for the reduction of the French strongholds in Corsica. For many months he was ashore commanding the naval brigade for the reduction of Bastia and Calvi; after it was all over he was angry and mortified to learn that owing to jealousy his part in the operations had been minimized by the general. But Hood, who knew what he had done, put matters right when he returned home.

Hood was succeeded by two commanders-in-chief of very different calibre, Hyde Parker and Hotham, and though they gave Nelson the independent command of the squadron operating with the Austrian army they never gave him sufficient ships. He did wonders with his far too weak squadron.

Then the redoubtable John Jervis arrived to take command. The other captains now hoped that all the plums would not fall to Nelson, but on their first meeting Jervis sized up Nelson and from that moment these two were fast friends. Nelson owed all his future appointments to Jervis, and Jervis owed a great deal to Nelson when he met the Spanish fleet off St Vincent.

Before that battle there was an incident that is specially noteworthy. Nelson had been sent with some frigates to evacuate the garrison at Elba. When he sailed from Gibraltar to join Jervis two Spanish battleships lying at Algeciras weighed and went in pursuit of the frigate. The frigate was managing to keep ahead of them when a man fell overboard. Nelson never hesitated, he backed the mizzen topsail and lowered a boat. The Spanish captains were so astonished that they did not take advantage of the situation. That night Nelson found himself in the presence of a Spanish squadron. He decided to shadow them, and to the dismay of the British Viceroy of Corsica, who was a passenger, to follow the squadron if necessary across the Atlantic. He knew it was of the greatest importance that the British government should know the destination of the squadron.

The Spanish squadron hauled up for Cadiz. Nelson rejoined the fleet, and took command of his new ship, the *Captain*. Would any other captain have stopped to pick up that man when two Spanish battleships were bowling down to attack? Would any other captain have sacrificed the chance of being present at a great battle in order to shadow those ships? These incidents exemplify his moral strength.

It was Nelson's brilliant tactic that won the Battle of St Vincent. There came a moment when he saw that the Spanish fleet would escape if something was not done to check their advance. He left the line and threw his ship against three far more powerful Spanish three-deckers.

Rigid rules governed tactics in those days. The fleet was in the command of a strict disciplinarian. Even though Nelson had virtually won the battle his action was severely criticized by other captains as inimical to discipline. John Jervis was far too great a man to take that view.

Then came the expedition for the capture of Teneriffe, for which Jervis, now Earl St Vincent, chose Nelson as commander. Nelson made most careful plans, which envisaged embarking 3700 soldiers from Gibraltar. The soldiers were not forthcoming, but Jervis thought the prize was worth taking a risk. The attack failed; Nelson lost his arm. He was terribly depressed, but the old Earl wrote and reminded him that mortals cannot command success and praised highly the gallantry of the attack.

Home then to be nursed by Fanny, and when his arm healed he returned as rear-admiral to St Vincent's fleet. When St Vincent was ordered to make his main objective the French fleet in Toulon, known to be preparing for a big operation, he chose Nelson over the heads of all the other rear-admirals for the command of a fleet in the Mediterranean. The other admirals were so loud in their protestations that Jervis ordered one of them home.

There followed the long search and the brilliant tactic which won the Battle of the Nile. During the long search Nelson explained his plans to his captains for every conceivable condition, and no signals were necessary when the French fleet was sighted. He was severely wounded in the head and saw little of the later stages. It was when he was ill and tired and wounded in the head—Saumarez, his second-in-command, wrote that he could not have borne the strain of the long search—that he became immersed in the affairs of the Sicilian Court.

Some biographers attempt to explain away his conduct during the next period. But the truth is that he became in his own words 'Sicilified' under the spell of Emma, the wife of the minister, and in the atmosphere of the dissolute Sicilian Court he abandoned his high standards. Twice he flatly refused to send his commander-in-chief— now Lord Keith—the ships, when it was Keith who was operating against the enemy fleet. Indeed, by his strange conduct he jeopardized the whole British position in the Mediterranean, and the Admiralty severely censured him. The constant references in his letters to the pains in his head go far to explain his conduct.

But if we draw a veil over this period, if we follow some biographies and search for plausible means to prove that Nelson, in making his only objective the propping up of the Sicilian king, to the exclusion of all else, including the French Mediterranean fleet, was far wiser than Lord Keith or the Admiralty, we miss one of the most remarkable incidents in Nelson's career.

The moment he set foot on English soil and was free from the scent-laden drawing-rooms of the European capitals and the flattery that had been such heady stuff, he applied for a command. He craved for the company of British sailors, and the salty tang of the sea winds. And the fact that he at once received an appointment which led to Copenhagen is a measure of his stature. For the goings-on at the Neapolitan Court were a subject of gossip in London and the talk of the European Court, and there were many influential people who held the view that though Nelson had won the Battle of the Nile his useful career was now over.

After Copenhagen came another example of his stature. Napoleon had assembled his invasion forces; the whole country was in a state of fear; the Prime Minister and St Vincent, now First Lord, asked Nelson to take command of the anti-invasion forces because he, and he alone, could restore confidence.

The invasion did not take place, and after Nelson was released from his command he spent the first peaceful and happy period of his life at Merton.

Then came a fresh summons to service when war again broke out. As commander-in-chief of the Mediterranean he conducted the long blockade, went on the long chase after the French fleet, and then finally met and defeated the combined Franco-Spanish fleet at Trafalgar.

I have dealt very briefly with this last period, because my purpose is to emphasize the lesser known incidents in his early life which reveal his moral strength.

When I left the *Victory* my search for Nelson came to an end. I had not found him, but he was no longer a remote, enigmatic, rather melodramatic figure; he had become to me a very human person. I had seen him walking the poop, sometimes with the faithful Dr Scott, discussing a letter from a foreign Court, sometimes with Hardy unravelling a knotty problem of supply, sometimes stopping to talk to a midshipman or sailor, often alone, turning over in his mind a new tactic, or with his thoughts far away at Merton. I had pictured him in his thin over-coat soaked after hours of walking in the rain, going to his cabin, taking off his buckled shoes and stockings and walking about bare-foot because he would not disturb his valet.

I had watched his guests going down the ladder to the tune of 'Roast Beef of England', some officers of the *Victory*, some from other ships, always some midshipmen, a merry company looking forward to a treat, a charming host, sparkling conversation, good food and wine. 'I dined with his Lordship last night and had a very merry dinner. He is certainly the pleasantest Admiral I ever served under', wrote one of his captains just before Trafalgar.

I knew now that the secret of his strength was that he understood plain men and was in turn understood by them. I often recall a passage in a letter written by a man who had stayed at Merton for several weeks:

Lord Nelson in private life was remarkable for a demeanour, quiet, sedate and unobtrusive, anxious to give pleasure to everyone about him, distinguishing each in turn by some act of kindness and chiefly those who seemed to require it most. During his few intervals of leisure, in a little knot of relatives and friends, he delighted in quiet conversation through which occasionally ran an undercurrent of pleasantry not unmixed with caustic wit. At his table he was the least heard amongst the company and so far from being the hero of his own tale I never heard him voluntarily refer to any of the great occasions of his life. In his plain suit of black in which he alone recurs to my memory he always looked what he was—a gentleman.

I knew that was the real Nelson, but, though no longer remote, I could never find him. His shipmates and intimate friends may have come near to understanding the secret of his magic power over his fellow-men but as our experience tells us there is nothing more baffling to analyse than personality. The light word that took their hearts in thrall, the golden look that welcomed them, his grace, his charm, and his courtesy, his boyishness, these we can never recapture.

Great victories on land and sea evoke admiration and respect for the victorious commander-in-chief, only seldom do they evoke affection or love.

It is Nelson's occasional indiscipline, his so human fits of depression when frustrated or over-tired, his eager response to friendly advances, his warm and enduring affection for senior officers who befriended him when he was an unknown young man, his sheer joy in meeting and overcoming difficulties, his magnetic influence over all who served with him, and his illicit and unswerving love for Emma Hamilton that evoke such a warm response from ordinary men and women. They feel he must have been so human and so understanding; they are drawn to him by his frailties. They think of him not only as the greatest sailor in history but as a great lover and an approachable, friendly, generous, human being.

The word friend appears more frequently in his letters than any other word. The great Duke would have greeted an acquaintance with two fingers; Nelson would have extended his whole hand.

It is not easy to compile a list of the qualities that contribute to the making of a great sea officer—no list would receive universal support—but there are some qualities he certainly must have: moral courage, endurance to resist strain and fatigue, imagination and creative powers for his strategical and tactical plans—and he must be a fine seaman. Nelson's moral courage was superb. The boy who insisted on joining the Arctic expedition was the father of the young captain who single-handed fought against the black market; who went on board the flagship after the battle of Toulon to beg an easily satisfied admiral to pursue the enemy; and of the fleet commander who discarded battle tactics, which if not ingenious were safe, to play for higher stakes. His physical energy was most remarkable. Throughout his long campaigns he was never off duty for a single day, and he would stand long hours in open boats in all weathers without a thought of the cold and discomfort. The third quality, imagination and creative powers, is the one which dictates the stature of an admiral.

The Nile shattered Napoleon's dream of an Eastern Empire; Copenhagen removed the threat of powerful fresh forces making common cause with the enemy when Britain was fighting alone and only just holding her own; after the defeat of the combined fleet off Cape Trafalgar Napoleon's army of invasion broke camp and headed

East. The tactical plans for each of these battles was a masterpiece. Nelson had a more difficult task than his successors who commanded fast-moving steam-driven fleets, because if his plans of approach had been faulty he could not remedy them by signal. Once his ships were locked in deadly combat he could do no more; no signal could be seen through the smoke of battle; nor could ships with broken spars and tattered sails respond, even if the momentary lull gave a glimpse of the flagship's masts.

With the rounding of the shoal of Aboukir Bay by the leading ship the die was cast; there could be no withdrawal at Copenhagen after the first broadside had been fired; once the leading ships of the columns at Trafalgar had swung round to the signal 'bear up and sail large' the pattern of the battle was decided. Some magic guided Nelson's hands as he pored over the charts and pencilled-in the tracks to be followed by his ships, but it was not the magic of sudden inspiration. All his battle plans were the result of long study. In whatever posture he found an enemy fleet he had a plan, and a plan that was known to all his captains.

The quality of being skilled in seamanship has been denied him by some biographers, but they are wrong. Whether he was in command of a frigate or a battleship or a fleet he won the admiration and sometimes the astonishment of his shipmates and fleetmates by his skill at handling ships in all weathers and in narrow and in badly charted waters.

Of the long blockade a British minister wrote: 'To have kept your ships afloat, your rigging standing, your crews in health and spirits, is an effort such as has never been realized in former times, nor I doubt will ever again be repeated by any other Admiral.' He was undoubtedly one of the greatest seamen that ever commanded a British fleet.

The power to draw loyalty and whole-hearted service from subordinates has not been included as a fundamental quality, as there have been successful admirals who have governed through their subordinates' fear of the consequences of failure. But Nelson's extraordinary influence over his fellow-men was perhaps as much responsible for his unique record of success in battle as his brilliant tactics. As he stepped on board ship some magnetic power radiated from him, morose men became gay-hearted, sluggards came alive, In a trice a motley collection of men with no common purpose became a band of brothers, and this wonderful power radiated far beyond his own ship and was felt in every ship in his fleets.

What would the future have held for him if that bullet had not proved fatal? No more battling on the grand scale, because with Trafalgar the major operations died away. He would have returned to England. The King, the ministers, the people, would have insisted on his return so that they could pay homage to the man who had dispelled the fears of invasion which had been gnawing at them ever since Napoleon had begun to assemble troops on the Channel coast. What would have followed the drives through London and other cities, the presentations of freedoms and swords of honour, the thanks of the Lords and Commons?

Sir William Hamilton's death had left him free to marry Emma; she was no light-of-love to Nelson. His love for her had stood the test of the strong disapproval of the highest in the land and his oldest friends; it would endure to the end. The social world that had looked askant at the liaison would have opened its doors wide to Earl and Countess Nelson.

We know from the post-mortem report that he was an extremely well-preserved man and would probably have lived to a great age. We know too, from his letters, how he craved for peace and quiet and a home-life surrounded by his friends and how he looked forward to watching Horatia blossom into womanhood, but it was not to be. If he had to die in battle there could have been no more fitting place than in the ship wearing his flag as vice-admiral of the White, and no more fitting moment than at the hour of victory. He died knowing that the fleet he had led in the battle and the men he loved had won a great victory; the last sound he heard was the distant rumble of a broadside; his last order 'Anchor' was the order of a great seaman; his last thoughts were for the woman he loved; his last words were 'God and my Country'.

Robert Louis Stevenson wrote of the British admirals: 'Their sayings and doings stir the English blood like the sound of a trumpet, and if the Indian Empire, the trade of London, and all the outward and visible ensigns of our greatness should pass away we should still leave behind us a durable monument of what we were in the sayings and doings of the English Admirals.' As the years roll on the pages of history become more and more congested. Except for a student of history, the events of whole centuries are packed into a few pages. Events that were cataclysmic to those who witnessed them shrink with the passage of years and even the names of those who moulded the destiny of nations fade into obscurity. There thus may come a day when Howe, Rodney, John Jervis, Hood and their rich achievements will be familiar only to a few who take up the study of the particular period in which they made history. But Nelson will never fade out of the pages of history. His sayings and doings are a durable monument, in very truth.

CHAPTER III

THE NAVY IN THE TWO WORLD WARS

For a hundred years after the defeat of Napoleon there was no serious threat to our sea-lines of communication, which became more and more important as our possessions overseas were developed and we became more and more dependent on sea-borne imports—food and raw materials. But the Navy was not idle. There were numerous wars in which the Navy supported the Army; the Crimea, during which three able seamen won the first three naval Victoria Crosses helping to save the Guard's colours at Inkerman; the Indian Mutiny, in which Peel's naval brigade achieved fame; two wars in China, numerous small wars in Africa, and finally the Boer War, in which naval brigades and naval guns played an important part. There was a time at the end of the nineteenth century when it seemed that our quarrels with France would lead to war, and we built and trained our Navy for war with France; but the threat faded away.

In shipbuilding the nineteenth century was a groping period. Naval architects were groping to produce a well-balanced fighting ship propelled by steam and built of steel. For many decades the solution evaded them. During the Crimea there was one squadron of sailing line of battleships and one squadron of sailing battleships fitted with screw propulsion. The architects were not prepared to sacrifice sail power or rely on steam only, and so they designed many ships that could neither sail nor steam. There were iron ships with massive masts and yards and guns placed in odd positions, followed by ships with very low freeboard, difficult to handle and poor fighting ships, and it was not until the end of the century that a well-balanced fighting ship reappeared, a ship with powerful guns on the fo'c'sle and quarter-deck and a battery of medium guns; and that type endured for many years. The Russo-Japanese War was fought with ships of that type, and it was during that war that the only case—except Quiberon Bay—of annihilation of a fleet occurred. The Russian fleet, carrying deck cargoes of coal and lumbering out to the Far East, was encountered in the Straits of Tsushima by the Japanese fleet of about equal strength in ships and guns but immensely superior in fighting efficiency and the whole Russian fleet was destroyed.

Then came the day when at the instigation of Lord Fisher the first Dreadnought was designed and the German people, strong, ambitious, and coveting the overseas possessions of other European nations, were glad to seize the chance of challenging British sea power. All earlier ships were rendered obsolete or obsolescent, and so the Germans, who hitherto were far behind Great Britain in the strength of their fleet, could start building a new fleet on level terms.

It has been said that by designing the Dreadnought Lord Fisher lost our supremacy and gave the Germans their chance, but in fact the Dreadnought as a type—a ship with all big guns—had become inevitable. The early years of this century witnessed a most remarkable advance in the development of the fighting power of ships. Guns that missed the target more often than they hit it at 2000 yards, in a very few years were hitting more often than they were missing at 20,000 yards. Torpedoes which ran a short distance and very often crooked were manufactured to run straight for ten miles. The last of the pre-Dreadnought ships mounted three types of guns, 12, 9·2 and 6 in., and it had become almost impossible to control accurately the fire of these guns at long range. It was almost impossible to distinguish between the fall of shot from the three types. For that reason only a ship with a single type of gun became inevitable.

It was not long before the nations of the world realized the intentions of the Kaiser and his advisers. For what purpose could the Germans require a great fleet as well as a great army? There could be only one purpose: when they had built up a fleet which could challenge our fleet, and when they had deepened the Kiel Canal, they would certainly throw down the gauge. And so a race began, and for the first time in our history the threat was so obvious that our government was prepared to spend the vast sums of money necessary to keep pace with German expansion. There was a time when the government wilted, but then the slogan ran round the country 'We want eight and we won't wait', and the building went on.

Concurrently with the building up of the Dreadnought fleet was the building of many new types—light cruisers, destroyers, submarines—and a great development in battle tactics. By the time war broke out we were able to deploy a very powerful and well-balanced fleet to contain the German fleet. The German fleet was only slightly inferior, and if by successful submarine operations or other means some of our battleships were put out of action, the Germans would have been able to meet our Grand Fleet on equal terms.

The strategy of the First World War was the strategy of the Seven Years War. The main fleet took up its position at Scapa Flow, from which it could contain the German fleet. In the five Oceans, cruiser squadrons kept the lines of communication open and slowly cleared the seas of many of the German ships deployed for attack on our trade.

By his victory off the Falkland Islands Admiral Sturdee removed a serious menace to our trade and in due course all German ships overseas were brought to battle and our distant sea-lines were made safe.

During the years previous to the war, we, and indeed all European countries, had become more and more dependent on the arrival of cargoes from overseas, we, of course, being the most sensitive to any interruption of our sea-borne commerce.

We were strong enough and so based that we could hold in check any German attack by major war vessels on our trade-routes, but for the first time in maritime history our enemy was able to exploit a new weapon against our trade for which it took a very long time to find and develop a counter-weapon.

By international law a merchant ship was not to be sunk before the crew had taken to the boats and unless those boats were within a reasonable distance of land. We did not anticipate that any belligerent would be so barbarous as to disregard this law. But in 1915 the Germans declared a policy of sinking without warning. By December they had sunk four hundred ships and counter-measures—indicator nets, 'Q' ships and small units equipped for anti-submarine warfare—were not holding their own. Then the sinking of the *Lusitania*, when a number of American lives were lost, roused the wrath of the American people. The Germans modified the instructions to their submarines, although American anger against the submarines was to a great extent balanced by their anger against our blockade. We were determined to use our sea power to its fullest extent and stop every ship destined for German ports, and this blockade was soon being felt in Germany; bread-rationing, indeed, began in February 1915. But there were serious sources of disagreement between us and other nations about what was contraband and what was not contraband, what we had the right to arrest on the high seas and what we should have to let pass into German ports.

It was in the next year, 1916, that the only battle between the main fleets took place. Despite the great strength of the German fleet, despite the opportunities of being able to sail unnoticed and of using high speed to evade, the German fleet was in the hands of men who had no intention of exploiting its great power, or of settling the issue by main battle. In May 1916 the whole German fleet put to sea. Their plan was to bombard the East Coast and draw the British fleet over a line of submarines. Admiral Scheer had no intention of being involved in major battle, but information of the sailing reached the British Admiralty and to Scheer's surprise he found himself in the presence of the British fleet. He had all the advantages: misty weather, which would enable his fleet to attack a part of the British fleet while the remainder of the British ships would be unable to engage, and his bases close by so that any damaged ships could make port.

But from the moment the British fleet was reported his one idea was to escape. Jellicoe's handling of the fleet was masterly. But there was little difference between the speeds of the two fleets and in the misty weather the German fleet was able to make good its escape. This half-begotten battle was a terrible disappointment to the British fleet and the British nation, but for the Germans it was disastrous. Though they lost few ships they never emerged again from their ports, and a rot set in amongst the personnel which culminated in the mutiny that heralded the end. If the Germans had understood how to wield sea power; if they had accepted that the issue would be decided by the main fleets under whose cover all the other operations were taking place; if they had risked something to give battle on the Jutland bank; then the war might have taken a very different turn.

Meanwhile, our blockade of Germany became more and more severe. Simultaneously, the German submarines were operating in greater and greater numbers, and the counter-measures were still far behind. The

whole interest of 1917 turned on the submarine campaign. In January the success of our blockade persuaded
Germany that victory must be won now or never. The
army could promise no immediate decision, the naval
experts promised victory within six months if they could
set aside all submarine restrictions. It was expected that
America would enter the war, but it was thought that the
American influence in the first six months would be
ineffective. In the Napoleonic War, the whole issue
depended on the British fleet, now once again the issue
depended on the British sailor but this time supported by
the British scientist.

The decision to put all resources into the submarine
campaign nearly brought Germany victory. Had the
loss of merchantmen been as heavy in May and June as
in April, the shortage of food and raw materials would
have become extremely serious for Great Britain. Before
the year's end starvation would have brought collapse,
just when French morale was low, Italy temporarily
collapsed, Russia out of the war and America not effec-
tively in. But a most remarkable combination of the
British sailor and scientist just managed to turn the corner
in time. 'Q' ships, depth charges, mines, dazzle painting,
and above all the convoy system, which became practic-
able when the entry of America made an immediate
augmentation of escort vessels possible and provided
ports for the assembly of vessels, slowly but steadily
reduced the sinkings. Despite the loss of 2500 ships
during the year the menace had been lifted by
December.

Meanwhile, the blockade of the Central Powers reached perfection and was as destructive to health and life in Germany as the German air raids or passenger sinkings had been to us.

It was thus sea power which played a decisive part in the collapse of the Central Powers, and it was sea power which enabled the great armies to pass over to France and be nourished for the great campaigns against the German army.

I referred in my first lecture to something that Lloyd George wrote about the Grand Fleet. There were a great many people in high places who, because there was no battle, could not or would not understand that the whole of our war effort hinged on the Grand Fleet. Because the Germans did not venture to exploit the power of their high sea fleet it did seem that the enormous battle power accumulated in that $7\frac{1}{2}$ miles of capital ships was wasted. But if Jellicoe had mishandled the situation at Jutland, or if during certain periods when, owing to dockings and accidents, the British fleet was reduced, the Germans had seized the opportunity to put the issue to the final test, the war might have taken a very different course. All the anti-submarine forces were working under the cover of the main fleet. With that fleet weakened the German battle cruisers and battleships could have been out on the trade-routes, and not a convoy could have sailed. One capital ship coming across a large convoy could sink the whole lot in a very short time.

Though the principles had not changed, something new and formidable had appeared. In an age of scientific development it had been possible to produce a new weapon—unrestricted submarine warfare was virtually a new weapon—for which it had taken a long time to find the adequate counter-weapon, and if that time had been a little longer the new weapon would have been decisive.

The advent of this new factor into maritime war, the power of a new weapon, caused much difficulty to those responsible for defence during the first years after the war. There was a campaign started by well-meaning people, and supported by a press baron, to abolish all armed ships, on the grounds that the issue would be entirely decided by the submarine. That campaign faded out when it was realized that the claims made for the submarine were nonsensical, but it was replaced by another campaign to persuade our people that the Navy was no longer their main defence because of the growing powers of the aeroplane. This campaign prospered under the guidance of a press baron and the extremists became quite wild in their claims. For instance it was stated many times on the platform that 1000 aeroplanes could be added to our defence system for one battleship because an aeroplane cost £10,000 and a battleship £1,000,000. That of course was an extremely attractive proposition to lay before our people. Some of the factors omitted from this calculation were that the useful life of a battleship is five or six times that of an aeroplane, that the cost of the air maintenance staff was very large, and that a battleship includes its stores and armaments.

The campaign was so successful, however, that eventually a Cabinet Committee was set up to inquire into the matter. The first thing that the Cabinet Committee discovered was that we could have only thirty-seven medium bombers for one battleship. The Committee was dumbfounded when this figure was produced for them and they also discovered, which should surely have been apparent to those conducting the campaign, that if we had no capital ships commensurate with the capital ships of our enemy, our enemy would send his ships to the St Lawrence, the Plate and the focal trade points and arrest the whole of our seaborne commerce. No plane then in existence could reach them or for that matter carry any weapons that could do them much damage. Other maritime nations were astounded at the success of this propaganda, more particularly as we were utterly dependent on seaborne imports, and their response was to hasten the building of more warships.

Our sensitiveness to interruption of our seaborne imports was increasing every year. All our fighting forces and our transport were becoming more and more dependent on oil, and every drop of oil had to be brought into the country. We were also importing every year more and more food and more and more of those metals which are necessary for modern factories, but which we cannot produce in our own country.

It was in this era, when we were becoming increasingly vulnerable, that our ability to defend our seaborne imports was slowly whittled away because of our belief that we were living in a new world in which international quarrels would be settled peaceably. It is far beyond my purpose to discuss the political history of the period, but

I must point out that our defence history passed through four stages during the inter-war years.

From 1920 to 1922 there was no possible threat to our sea-lines and the people, represented by Parliament and the Press, were determined to reduce drastically the money spent on defence.

Then in the period 1922–6 the Geddes Axe and other inquisitions, followed by the Ten-year Rule which laid down that there could be no war for ten years, resulted in a soporific effect on the administration of the fighting services, in the destruction of many of the war industries and the loss of skilled men. Then came the third stage— 1926–32—when it was so obvious that the Navy had to be rebuilt that some money was forthcoming. There were international conferences attended by the principal maritime Powers which we hoped would result in a general agreement to scale down naval armaments. The fourth stage, 1934–8, saw the slow and cumbrous effort to re-arm. It was slow and cumbrous because so many of the factories which could once produce arms were now non-existent, and because there were so few men skilled in the art of making guns, armaments and everything that goes to make a ship.

When the war clouds again gathered we had sufficient surface ships of the battleship and cruiser type to contain German ships of the same types. If, as was expected, Mussolini plunged his country into war when confident that Hitler's military operations were prospering, our Mediterranean fleet, in co-operation with the French fleet, could contain the Italian main fleet. We could not afford to send a fleet of any strength to Eastern waters should Japan seize the opportunity to realize her long-cherished dreams of wide conquest in the Pacific. But we hoped that if she did wage a war of aggression the powerful American navy would intervene.

Our trade-route defence was in better shape than at the outset of the First World War, because we were ready to throw into gear a full convoy system. Moreover, despite financial restrictions, the study of anti-submarine devices and tactics had never relaxed. But as the available money had perforce been devoted to building the ships that take many years to build we were not well off in convoy escort vessels. The unknown factors were the influence of the aeroplane on maritime war and the possibility of the sudden appearance of a secret weapon.

Our strategic dispositions were the same as in earlier wars, and for the same purpose. We required command of the narrow seas to pass our army to France, and we had to bring to battle as soon as possible German surface vessels operating on our trade-routes. We had to afford the maximum protection to the ocean convoys. On the night of 3 September 1939 the liner *Athenia* was sunk without warning 250 miles west of Ireland, and we knew that the Germans had no intention of honouring the signature which they had affixed in 1936 to the submarine warfare protocol.

In December Commodore Harwood brought the battleship *Graf Spee* to action off the River Plate. His squadron consisted of one 8 in. and two 6 in. ships. This is one of the strangest battles in maritime history. The powerfully armed and armoured German ship could have destroyed the 8 in. cruiser at long range, ignoring the 6 in. ships. But after putting the 8 in. ship out of action she ran for the River Plate, chased by the 6 in. ships. She appeared again only to scuttle herself.

Up to the end of the year the submarine attack was not causing concern, but a matter of grave concern was the appearance of a secret weapon—the magnetic mine. Large numbers of these mines were laid at night by aeroplane in all our southern estuaries, and soon all shipping was brought to a standstill. For a short period we were in grave danger. We had lost control of the sea-routes. Then when the situation looked very black two of the mines were washed up in the Thames estuary. The secret was ours, but a colossal effort was necessary to render these mines, and their successors the acoustic mine, impotent. No less than 1200 miles of wire cable were being wound weekly to demagnetize ships, and in a few months a mine-sweeping force of 76 ships and 2000 personnel had expanded to 320 ships and 10,000 personnel.

By April 1940 the menace from the first secret weapon had abated; there were only a few armed German merchant ships at large in the oceans; and though the German submarine campaign had prospered, our control of the sea-routes was not so far materially weakened. Control of the ocean-routes was becoming more important as every month passed. It was our sea power which in earlier wars had enabled us to lengthen the striking distance of our armies after we had wrested control of the sea-routes from the enemy; now it was more important than ever to be free to send armies and air forces where we wished to exploit their power. At first it was the strengthening of overseas garrisons that was important, but soon the Navy was called on to shepherd great convoys carrying troops from the British Isles and the Dominions to the Middle East, and great convoys carrying Canadian troops to the British Isles.

If our control had weakened, if it had become too hazardous to embark troops for ocean voyages, we could never have held our position on the Egyptian frontier, and at a later stage German and Italian armies would have found their way to Syria, to Persia, to the Caucasus, and perhaps to India, open and undefended.

Never before had such vast movements of seaborne armies been carried to a successful conclusion. Between September 1939 and December 1944 over ten million troops were carried over the ocean-routes in escorted convoys, and only 2848 were lost at sea. That was sea power expressing itself in full measure.

With the coming of April the maritime war entered a new phase. The Germans invaded Denmark and Norway. This move found us quite unprepared. It is difficult to understand why that was so. Many who had made a study of war—Sir Herbert Richmond, late Master of Downing College, Cambridge, for instance—had forecast this invasion as the correct strategy for the Germans: securing their flank before advancing westwards. Our attempts to stem the German advance were doomed to failure from the outset. We had command of the sea-lines to Norway, but we had not the troops or air forces necessary to oppose the powerful German forces. Early in June the last of our troops were re-embarked. In the two battles off Narvik our destroyers had sunk seven of the German's most modern destroyers and a submarine had sunk a German light cruiser; these German ships if well handled could have been a serious menace to our sea-lines in the narrow seas. But we lost two cruisers and four destroyers and more important the aircraft carrier *Glorious*, sunk by the German battle cruisers when homeward bound with no covering force. That loss was due to too many cooks stirring the ether. There should have been only one senior officer giving orders in the area; that short, ill-starred campaign was conducted on such strange lines that an Admiral-of-the-Fleet was afloat in Norwegian waters in a cruiser with his flag flying in the area of command of the C.-in-C. Home fleet: he arrived in Norway with orders diametrically opposite to the orders given to the general with whom he was to co-operate.

With his flank secure Hitler ordered his armies to march westward. Our control of the narrow seas enabled us to withdraw the British army but otherwise there was little that could be done, and when the Germans secured the French Atlantic ports the whole strategic situation was radically changed.

In the First World War the Germans lacked the third element—bases. Their submarines and surface ships, in order to attack our main trade-routes, had to complete a long outward passage through the North Sea, passing our main bases before operating, and a long homeward passage after operating. With the French ports in their possession their submarines and surface ships were only a short distance from the ocean-routes, and during the inter-war years we had abandoned our right to use the bases in South Ireland from which a watch could have been kept on the French ports.

As we anticipated, Mussolini declared war as soon as he felt confident that complete victory for the Germans would not be long delayed, and the maritime war entered a new phase. For the next three years the issue in the Western Hemisphere depended on our ability to exercise our sea power in the Atlantic and overcome the fierce, persistent attack on our seaborne trade by German surface ships and submarines, and to exercise our sea power in the Mediterranean to enable our armies to operate first against the Italian and then against the German armies.

It was our sea power that had caused the downfall of Napoleon; it was our sea power that caused the downfall of the Axis powers. Our army in the Nile delta and our army in Abyssinia could enjoy mobility only if ports on their flanks were open for seaborne supplies—food, water, ammunition, reinforcements—and a main commitment for the British fleet was to ensure the arrival of those supplies. As the battle in the desert swayed forward and backward the inshore squadrons fought through the coastal convoys. They suffered heavy losses from air attack and submarine but never failed in their task.

The defection of the French fleet had left the British fleet much inferior in all types of warships to the Italian fleet, but the fourth element—seamen—was lacking in that powerful fleet. Admiral Cunningham explained the principles that governed his conduct of the campaign: 'We started very weak at sea and even more so in the air. However, because of the very fact of our weakness our policy had obviously to be one of aggressiveness; and it paid handsome dividends.' It did pay handsomely. On many occasions the Italian fleet was in gunshot of far weaker British forces but when the British forces turned to attack the Italians retreated to their defended harbours. It was not the Italian fleet but the air weapon wielded by the Germans that severely threatened our power to keep open the sea-lines of communication.

Taking advantage of our control in the Eastern Mediterranean an army was conveyed to Greece. But by the time they were deployed powerful German forces had come to the aid of the incompetent Italian troops, and they were soon re-embarking for Crete. Enemy air forces were steadily increasing their influence in the narrow seas and the re-embarkation was achieved only by first-rate organization and good seamanship—but not without losses.

It was later, in the battle of Crete, that the Germans exploited the full power of the air weapon in narrow-sea warfare. We did not lose control of the sea-lines of communication, but our losses in cruisers and destroyers were on the scale of a major fleet action.

To add to these losses midget Italian submarines entered Alexandria and immobilized two battleships. Admiral Cunningham was left with only a handful of cruisers and destroyers to exercise sea power over a wide area, in face of an overpoweringly strong Italian fleet and the persistent attacks of the strong German air forces. But by indomitable courage and superb seamanship that small force kept open the sea-lines of communication on which our whole position in the Middle East rested. It was lack of the third element—bases—that had such an adverse influence on the operations of the British fleet. A most important commitment was the harassing of the Italian lines of communication to Africa. They were 1000 miles from Alexandria. These lines could be easily attacked from Malta but the enemy air attacks rendered that base of little value. Another commitment was the succouring of Malta; fighting through the convoys to Malta was a desperate business, but sufficient ships arrived to keep the island alive.

So in this long drawn out and fiercely fought Mediterranean campaign we never, despite heavy losses, lost control of the sea communications and so, when the time came for Montgomery to give the order to advance, the sea-road on his flank, by which must pass everything required to nourish his army, was open.

We had exercised our sea power in the Mediterranean against heavy odds; we encountered even heavier odds in exercising our sea power in the Atlantic. The Germans put all their faith in the submarine. They did reinforce the submarine attack from time to time by surface attack, but that was not the real menace. The *Scharnhorst* and *Gneisenau* did considerable damage on their one cruise but they were afterwards held in Brest by air attack and did no more; the *Bismarck* was sunk before she had done any damage.

It was by turning out submarines in very large numbers and by exploiting new methods of attack, made possible by higher speed, that our defence was so sorely tried. Indeed, it seemed at one period that we would lose control of our sea communications and lose the war.

The commitments for our naval forces in other seas increased as the submarine attack was pressed more and more vigorously. With the entry of Russia large forces had to be devoted to guarding the convoys to Archangel; despite heavy attacks we controlled that line of communication to the end. With the entry of Japan large forces were deflected from the West for the hopeless task of endeavouring to stem the Japanese advance to the South.

The American entry into the war was an assurance that we would continue to exercise our sea power in the Atlantic provided they could bring their strength into the battle in time, and gave new hopes that the Japanese advance would be arrested.

In the West it was indeed a race against time. The Americans were not organized or prepared to protect their shipping, and their entry was followed by some black months. The Germans seized their opportunity, and opened up a tremendous submarine offensive on the American seaboard. This was checked only after 250 ships had been sunk in sight of the coast.

Slowly but surely the combined American and British sea and air forces wrested the initiative from the submarines. When at last the long-range aeroplane and the special hunting squadrons were thrown into the battle the menace first abated and then almost vanished. But it is of special note that the menace was at its height when the Allies decided to accept the hazards of sending overseas to North Africa a great army—the operation which heralded the defeat of the Axis powers. That, like the decision to hold our position in Egypt, was a very courageous decision.

Once we were able to exercise our sea power to the full the war moved to its inevitable conclusion. Never before in the long history of maritime war has sea power been wielded in such majestic form as when 1000 ships carrying the allied armies weighed, turned to a southerly course, and passed unimpeded by the enemy down the swept Channel to Normandy.

With that great amphibious operation the maritime war in the West became fitful, and then died away.

It was sea power that wrested from the Japanese their widespread conquests and then made the Japanese homeland the final battlefield. The British fleet had never been powerful enough to fight in the Eastern and Western Hemispheres simultaneously, but it was possible to send a British fleet comprised of all the modern units to fight with the American fleet in the last stages. The magnitude and complexity of the amphibious operations in the Pacific; the large number of fleet actions and their decisive issue; the masterly strategy, the formidable supply problem for large forces fighting thousands of miles from main bases; these constitute an epic of sea fighting, perhaps the greatest and possibly the last.

It will therefore be seen that sea power was decisive in the Second World War. There were many new weapons by which sea power was exercised, particularly the aeroplane, both shore-based and ship-borne, but it was sea power which, by conferring freedom to use the sea-roads, decided the issue.

In the East, the severing of the Japanese sea-lines of communication to the Solomons and New Guinea heralded victory. In the West our enemy once again came nigh to severing our lines of communication but that fourth of the four elements—the men—the seaman and airman—wrested from the German submarines their once dominant position and eventually rendered them impotent. Of the other elements the Italians had a powerful fleet and the Germans had many powerful vessels with great potential power of injury to our shipping but their powers were never fully exploited. We were able to sweep off the oceans the Italian and German merchant navies. Never before in maritime history has the third element—bases—had such a forceful influence on the issue. The German acquisition of French Atlantic bases greatly increased the striking power of their weapons. Lack of a base nearer to Italian lines to Africa than Alexandria and Gibraltar seriously limited our offensive against those lines. On the other hand we were able to establish bases in the Atlantic from which aeroplanes could cover the main sea-routes. Without those bases we should have been hard put to it to abate the submarine menace.

Great changes have taken place in the last decade in the construction of warships, and I for one would not dare to forecast what a warship will look like twenty years hence. But until and unless some new weapon like the atom bomb renders completely obsolete all the weapons we have known, we still must have merchant ships, weapons to protect them, and bases and seamen if we are to exercise sea power, that is to say if we are to exist for more than a few days after a declaration of war.

During this century we have witnessed rapid development of the power and reach of weapons, but there have been two unchangeables—the infantry soldier and the merchant ship. The merchant ship has altered little in the last fifty years—it will alter little in the next fifty years. It must always be a commodious receptacle for bulk cargoes that can be propelled across the oceans economically. On that ship our existence depends. It is because ever since Tudor days we have been able to fashion and to build sufficient weapons to protect that ship from assault during her voyages both homeward with food and raw materials and outward with soldiers, that this small island is to-day the heart of a great Empire.

INDEX